BRIGHT NOTES

SATYRICON BY PETRONIUS

Intelligent Education

Nashville, Tennessee

BRIGHT NOTES: Satyricon
www.BrightNotes.com

No part of this publication may be used or reproduced in any manner whatsoever without written permission, except in the case of brief quotations in critical articles and reviews. For permissions, contact Influence Publishers http://www.influencepublishers.com.

ISBN: 978-1-645423-72-0 (Paperback)
ISBN: 978-1-645423-73-7 (eBook)

Published in accordance with the U.S. Copyright Office Orphan Works and Mass Digitization report of the register of copyrights, June 2015.

Originally published by Monarch Press.
Gareth L. Schmeling, 1971
2019 Edition published by Influence Publishers.

Interior design by Lapiz Digital Services. Cover Design by Thinkpen Designs.

Printed in the United States of America.

Library of Congress Cataloging-in-Publication Data forthcoming.
Names: Intelligent Education
Title: BRIGHT NOTES: Satyricon
Subject: STU004000 STUDY AIDS / Book Notes

CONTENTS

1) Introduction to Petronius — 1

2) Overview — 21

3) Characters In The Satyricon — 24

4) Reconstruction of The Plot — 28

5) Detailed Analysis — 30

6) Essay Questions and Answers — 57

7) Bibliography — 64

INTRODUCTION TO PETRONIUS

HIS LIFE, WORK, AND INFLUENCE

Today's avant-garde novelists, film-makers, playwrights, and poets have found inspiration and even a model in a first-century A.D. work called the *Satyricon* composed by the Roman Petronius. It is fair to say that this once hardly-known work has become one of the most popular and certainly one of the most influential books of our time. We aim here to show the student and the general reader why and how this has happened, and to enhance their personal experience of the *Satyricon*. We shall investigate the social and cultural conditions in Petronius' time, and observe the similarities between his age and ours; review in detail the content, style, and techniques of the *Satyricon* and comment on the reasons for its appeal to the modern reader; and supply numerous suggestions for further study of both Petronius and his modern disciples.

PETRONIUS' LIFE AND DEATH

In life and in death, Petronius seems both mysterious and contradictory. So far as we can ascertain, there are no specific autobiographical clues in his classic work, *Satyricon*. We have no information about the circumstances of his birth; a reasonable guess would be that he was born about 20 A.D. From evidence supplied by the Roman historian, Tacitus (c. 55 A.D.-c. 117 A.D.), we infer that Petronius died in 66 A.D. This account of Petronius' character and career is found in Tacitus' *Annales* (XVI 18–19):

During the day he slept, but at night he conducted his business and enjoyed life. While hard work often brings fame to some, Petronius became well known by his idleness. But through all this he was not considered a debauchee or profligate like many who waste their incomes; rather he was held to be a man of refined luxury. The freer and more careless his deeds and words were, the more they were admired for their look of natural simplicity. First as proconsul of Bithynia and then as consul, Petronius showed that he could be energetic and equal to any task. Then with another about-face, Petronius returned to his old vices or affectation of vice and was chosen to be a member of Nero's innermost circle of friends, where he soon was regarded as Arbiter of Elegance. Nero soon came to believe nothing delightful or charming unless Petronius first approved it. Because of Petronius' position of power with Nero, Tigellinus, prefect of the Praetorian Guard, became jealous of Petronius and viewed him as a rival and even his superior in the study and practice of pleasure. By playing on Nero's cruelty, his worst passion, Tigellinus aroused the emperor's suspicions and accused Petronius of having been a friend of the traitor Scaevinus. Next Tigellinus bribed one of Petronius' servants to give evidence against him, removed any recourse to defense, and imprisoned most of his staff and servants. At the same time that all this was happening, Nero was making his way to Campania. Petronius set out in that direction but was stopped when he had gone as far as Cumae. No longer would he torture himself with thoughts of fear and hope; neither would he recklessly throw away his life. After having cut his veins, he bound them up, only to open them again as the mood struck him. Further, he kept up conversations with his friends, not on serious topics like glory and courage. He asked his friends not to bore him with discussions of immortality and the thoughts of philosophers, but to read him light verses and love songs. While he had some of his servants flogged, to others he gave large gifts. He would sleep for awhile, then dine. Though death was forced on him, Petronius made it appear natural. While many of those compelled to commit suicide flattered Nero and Tigellinus in their wills in hope of gaining something, Petronius refused. In fact, Petronius made an exact list of all the sexual offenses of Nero, together with the names of his male and female partners, itemized which acts were particularly perverted, and sent the list under his own seal to Nero. He then broke his signet-ring so that it could not be used to endanger others.*

If Petronius believed in anything, it was a kind of Epicurean existence. He both lived well and died well. The two most famous Stoics of the day, Seneca and Lucan, who preached a fairly rigid morality and philosophized on living and dying, both lived and died poorly. Seneca, who extolled all virtues, grew rich under Nero, then flattered the emperor in lavish terms in hope of a longer life, and finally died quite unlike a good Stoic. Lucan, when implicated in a plot to kill Nero, named his own mother as one of the conspirators, in an attempt to get lenient treatment. Whereas Seneca and Lucan preached the proper living and dying, it was Petronius who followed through. Furthermore, Petronius' literary goals were totally opposed to those of Lucan and Seneca and he parodied some of their works in his *Satyricon*. Jeremy Taylor, the famous English cleric, in his *The Rule and Exercise of Holy Dying* (1651), comments very favorably on the character of Petronius.

---

* Translations from the Latin given in this Monarch Note are by the author, Professor Gareth Schmeling.

EXTANT WORK OF PETRONIUS

The *Satyricon* has suffered much in its passage from Petronius to us. We now possess a little more than two of the original twenty or so books of the *Satyricon*, and much of that, the *Cena Trimalchionis*, was not discovered until about 1640, when it was found at Trau in Dalmatia by Marinus Statileus. Sometime early in the Middle Ages, a copyist had made only excerpts of the *Satyricon*. Perhaps the length of the *Satyricon* prevented its coming down to us in its entirety. Except for the *Cena*, the excerptor chose just bits and pieces from the prose, while he preserved much of the poetry intact. The extant *Satyricon* runs to only about 35,000 words.

Form and Title of the *Satyricon*. In the broadest sense the form of the *Satyricon* is prosimetric, a melange of prose and verse. While the greatest share of the *Satyricon* is written in prose, there is a considerable amount of poetry: Petronius writes in at least nine different meters and includes two long poems, one of 65 lines and another of 295. This mixture of prose and verse was apparently first used in the third century B.C. by Menippus of Gadara as a vehicle for **satire**. The learned Roman Varro also used the form and from him it passed on to Seneca and Petronius. Seneca used the form of Menippean **satire**, in his Apocolocyntosis, a biting satire on the apotheosis of the emperor Claudius on his death in 54 A.D. After Petronius, Menippean **satire** was employed by Macrobius, Boethius, and Martianus Capella.

The Latin word satura, from where we derive our word **satire**, meant much more to the ancients than our word **satire** does to us. By satire we mean any type of literature directed toward the correction of vices by means of ridicule. To the Romans, satura meant a potpourri of **themes** or stories. Horace classified his Trip to Brundisium (**Satire** 1.5) as a satura. Therefore by designating the *Satyricon* as Menippean **satire** scholars do not mean to imply that the *Satyricon* is everywhere satiric. On the other hand, there is in the *Satyricon* much of what we would call **satire**. Throughout the ensuing discussion of the *Satyricon*, elements of **satire** will be noted as they arise.

Apparently there are at least three reasons why Petronius chose to entitle his novel the *Satyricon*. He wants to tell his readers that this is a work about satyrs. In classical mythology, satyrs were forest revelers who attended the deity Bacchus; in form they were conceived of a half-men, half-goats, and they were notoriously lustful. Of course, any Roman who was brutish and lascivious would be dubbed a satyr. Furthermore, in an early **episode** of the *Satyricon* there is much talk of satyricon, the most famous of Roman aphrodisiacs. Petronius loves such word-play and uses it throughout his work. Finally, of course, as we have noted, *Satyricon* is a satire. William Arrowsmith summed it up very neatly when he described the *Satyricon* as a book of "satyr-things satirically treated."

In its original form of twenty books, the *Satyricon* was one of the longest books written in the ancient world. But one should always keep in mind, when discussing ancient literature, that a work like the *Satyricon* was written to be read aloud, and then only one book at a time. Around Nero's imperial court had sprung up a literary circle to which Petronius would read his new work. *The Cena Trimalchionis*, or *Banquet of Trimalchio*, is the subject treated in Book 15, the whole of which can be read aloud in a little more than one hour. Nero was very much interested in literature and tried to promote young talent. At court there developed a coterie of literary talent to rival that at the court of Augustus: Seneca, Persius, Lucan, and Petronius. Before Nero became completely deranged and totally under the influence of the corrupt Tigellinus, he was a true patron of the arts. But his better instincts gave way to evil and he became jealous of the fame of Seneca and Lucan. Seneca withdrew from the public eye, but it was not enough. Lucan was forbidden to publish anything. Finally Nero became jealous of Petronius. All three paid for their talent with their lives. Persius, luckily, died young.

BURLESQUE

Burlesque is the term used for the literary form in which both people and their actions are made ridiculous through incongruity. In Petronius, everything and anything is proper subject material for burlesque. Organized religion and religious superstition are frequently attacked. In this Petronius shares the Epicurean's dislike for transcendental deities. The growing class of nouveau riche - especially former slaves and freedmen from the eastern empire, who by wise investment and unscrupulous means stumbled to prominence outside the best circles - is constant grist for the Petronian mill. Trimalchio, the most famous character in the *Satyricon*, is one of this class, and Petronius, rather than trying to condemn Trimalchio's lowest-class manners, allows Trimalchio to put himself down and thus produce a **parody** of himself. No class of women fares well at the hands of Petronius: faithful wives always prove in the end to be unfaithful, priestesses are found to be a disgrace to organized religion, and the worst of vices are laid at the feet of even teenage girls. All female figures are portrayed in the first place as virtuous only to fall to the slightest temptation. And some, even at the time of emphasizing their own virtue, do not desist from entering into shameful alliances. No matter how degenerate, they continue to profess their goodness. Petronian **burlesque** consists largely of delineating characters who practice the opposite of what they preach. Government officials, who consistently point up what great public-works projects they have undertaken, are open to all types of bribes. Teachers and poets, claiming to be instruments of transmission of higher values, fall to the lowest depths of fawning, flattering, and deceit.

It seems preferable to term the *Satyricon* a **burlesque** rather than a **satire**. Satire is properly defined as the art of diminishing a subject and evoking toward it an attitude of contempt. There is a good deal of evidence to support the theory that Petronius in his **burlesque** (a literary form in which people and their actions are made ridiculous) does not mean to condemn or diminish his characters, but merely to derive as many humorous situations as possible from each scene.

EPIC AND MOCK-EPIC

Throughout the *Satyricon* the hero or rather anti-hero, Encolpius (Greek name meaning "in the crotch"), compares himself to Odysseus who was forced by the god Poseidon to wander over the Mediterranean world because of certain offences done to him. In the *Satyricon* Encolpius travels from Marseilles in France to Croton in southern Italy, hounded all the while by Priapus, an eastern fertility god. As he is driven from place to place, Encolpius tries to appease Priapus so that he, like Odysseus, might find a place to call home. Of course the troubles of Encolpius are a comic take-off on the tragic events in the life of Odysseus. There are several scenes in the *Satyricon* which **parody episodes** in the *Odyssey* and which Petronius intends to be mock-epic. Since the *Odyssey* was the most famous adventure story in the ancient world, Petronius could count on his audience to see the **parody** of the Homeric epic.

ROMANCE OR NOVEL

The proper **genre** designation of the *Satyricon* is either romance or novel. The essential difference between romance and novel lies in the delineation of characters. The romance tends to create stylized characters in a kind of fairyland, while the novel portrays realistic persons in a natural setting. But this division seldom remains firm, and one man's novel is another man's romance. Since the *Satyricon* is an extended narrative but cannot come under such general rubrics as history or essay, it is best to designate it a novel, a term more in common use than romance. It is proper to point out, however, that because the *Satyricon* stands at the very beginning of the history of the novel, it lacks a well-wrought plot, consistency, and objectivity. For Petronius, events need not always have antecedents, and stylized characters reveal a degree of subjectivity to which the twentieth-century audience is not accustomed. Because the characters move in such a subjective sphere, the world they populate takes on the atmosphere of a fairyland and appears to be closer to an imaginative setting than a real location.

The *Satyricon* is written in the first person, and from that fact arises no end of scholarly discussion. Most of the trouble occurs when readers try to determine if and when Encolpius, the first-person narrator, ever speaks for Petronius or echoes Petronian sentiments. As readers go through the *Satyricon*, they must constantly ask themselves whether it is Petronius himself who is reproaching contemporary Roman manners, or a narrator of such low repute that the reproach is vitiated.

To the early Greeks and Romans, the only medium for imaginative literature was poetry. Men of serious literary purpose avoided prose. Even the early Greek philosophers expressed their ideas in poetry, and Hesiod in writing Works and Days, a manual for farmers, employed verse. Only history and philosophy were regularly set down in prose.

    Imaginative prose literature can be said to originate with Herodotus (480–425 B.C.), whose Histories are full of short stories and digressions, written more for entertainment and edification than for data-processing. History for entertainment was continued by Xenophon (430–355 B.C.), especially in his *Cyropaedia* (Education of Cyrus), in which he narrates the love story of Panthea and Abradatas. After the death of Alexander the Great (323 B.C.), whose deeds and life inspired both soldiers and writers, there arose, beginning with Callisthenes (d. 327 B.C.), a whole series of romances (in part historical but mostly imaginative) on the exploits of the young conqueror. Like Odysseus, the greatest of all the heroes, Alexander traveled to exotic places and performed superhuman deeds, all of which captured the imagination of those writing at that time. In the plays of Euripides (480–406 B.C.) and Menander (342–292 B.C.), in the *New Comedy*, and in the poetry of Callimachus (b. 310 B.C.) of Alexandria there are the seeds of a new literary **genre**, that of sentimental romance. Certain plays of Euripides and of Menander, together with the short sketches of love stories by Alexandrian poets and Parthenius, molded at least the outlines of a genre which would dwell primarily on the subjective feelings and erotic (not pornographic) actions of a pair of lovers. A group of historians, interested now in artistic effect only, were influenced by (1) dramatic **themes** from comedy and tragedy, (2) love-elegies of Callimachus and others, (3) prose paraphrases of love stories by Parthenius and others, and incorporated them into their histories. Travel adventures (Reiseromanen) like the *Odyssey*, the *History of Alexander*, and various other Reiseromanen from Alexandria, plus sentimental love stories, combined to produce what we call romance. The main elements of romance were, and are today, travel and love.

Though this new form, which evolved into our modern novel, was regarded by the literate aristocracy in antiquity to be on a low and disreputable level of literature, it did find a home in the popular imagination of the rising middle-class, which was interested in the private concerns of the individual apart from society and in men and women as individuals, not imperfect copies of the gods.

PROSE FICTION

If poetry is the language of aristocrats, then prose is the language of the common man. As the common man emerged from obscurity into a type of middle-class man, there was a need for entertainment suitable for him. Aristocracy-oriented poetry would not work. Moreover, the prose fiction of romance dealt with love, adventure, and tales of wonder. It meant to entertain, not edify, chastise, or correct; its acceptance in the pre-Christian Roman Empire was assured. The aristocracy and the literati of the ancient world, together with the literary critics, never accepted or even acknowledged prose fiction. In his *Poetics* Aristotle clearly points out that fiction belonged to the realm of poetry, and history to prose. It is to the writings of ancient history that the student of the novel must always turn when seeking sources. As history evolved in the ancient world, it did not tend toward scientific exactness, a truly modern concept, but toward retelling the new, the marvelous, and the curious. History became dramatic and stressed **themes** with a visual impact. When history made use of erotic **themes** in extended digression, prose fiction - that is, romance - was born.

WRITERS OF FICTION

Seven relatively complete romances survive to our time, five Greek and two Latin. In addition to Petronius' *Satyricon*, written in Latin, there is Apuleius' (c. 125–190 A.D.) *The Golden Ass* or *Metamorphoses*, the story of the change of Lucius into an ass, his return to human form, and finally his ordination into the priesthood of Isis. The earliest of the five Greek romance-writers is Chariton (1st century A.D.) whose Chaereas and Callirhoe concerns the separation and final union of the two central figures. Xenophon of Ephesus (early 2nd century A.D.) wrote his Ephesiaca in apparent imitation of Chariton's flowing and easy style. The four above-mentioned romances develop their plots around love themes. The **episodes** only incidentally belong to a central plot, but since all the action revolves around one character, or two at the most, there is a kind of built-in unity. All novels must be extended narratives, and this is achieved in these four novels by moving the characters from place to place and piling **episode** on episode in each location. The same method is employed by Henry Fielding in *Tom Jones*. Longus' *Daphnis and Chloe*, probably the best known of all ancient romances, is different in that the travel element of the travel-love structure is missing. The plot of *Daphnis and Chloe* centers around the discovery of pastoral love by Daphnis and Chloe. Longus, dated to the late 2nd century, is a contemporary of Achilles Tatius, the author of *Leucippe and Clitophon*. Achilles Tatius departs from the strictly sentimental romance and incorporates several erotic **episodes** into his story. The longest and best constructed Greek romance is the *Aethiopica of Heliodorus* (early 3rd century A.D.), a slightly erotic tale about the adventures and misadventures of Theagenes and Chariclea.

PICARESQUE NOVEL

Many contend that the picaresque novel developed first in Spain during the 16th century. Picaro is Spanish for "rogue," and the typical picaresque novel concerns the exploits of a rogue hero who lives by his wits. Such a rogue in modern novels is often termed an anti-hero. If, however, the *Satyricon* is viewed primarily as an account of the life and actions of its narrator, Encolpius, then it should rank as the earliest picaresque novel. Petronius refuses to pass judgment on the indecent deeds of Encolpius, neither approving nor condemning. Most novels have heroes whose actions are basically those approved of by society. The anti-hero performs actions which are not accepted openly in society, but which, when related with skill, draw at least begrudging approval. While the anti-hero lives and acts at variance with accepted codes, he is often admired for his individuality. Like every picaro after him, Encolpius lives in accordance with his own peculiar mores only. Note here the similarity to Captain Yossarian in Joseph Heller's Catch-22 (1960) or to Sebastian Dangerfield in J. P. Donleavy's Ginger Man (1956). Petronius' use of an anti-hero is surely a major reason for his popularity today.

LEVELS OF INTENT

There is no inherent fallacy in seeking an answer to the question: "What is the intent of the author in writing the *Satyricon?*" There is, of course, no single answer, as every reader must, in the light of his own past experience, determine what the writer has to say to him. There are three general approaches to Petronius taken by critics and scholars. There are those who consider Petronius to be a corrupt debauchee at Nero's court, writing to titillate the emperor and his friends. Early Christian writers placed Petronius in this category. Then there are those who believe Petronius to be just the opposite of this; that is, they feel he is a moralist who writes about the vices of men merely to show how bad they are. Certain of these who consider Petronius to be a moralist, also hold that he is an Epicurean with a cynical and detached view of life. The third group of critics sees in Petronius only an artist, a writer trying to create an object of art. They believe that Petronius is a literary opportunist who writes for maximum effect and chooses **themes** with the most possibilities, themes which allow the greatest freedom for his virtuosity.

PETRONIAN LATIN STYLE

The Latin of Petronius is strikingly different from anything else which survives of Latin literature. It is at once easy and studied. In the ages after Cicero (106–42 B.C.), when formal rhetoric took a firm hold on Latin literature, creative writers of all **genres** came under its stifling influence. Styles became overblown, verbose, and in general artificial; literature had lost its naturalness, and style its grace. The production of literary works became a kind of academic exercise: history could not offend the emperor; drama was written to be read, not performed; **epic** was derivative, manufactured in the study, not inspired by heroes. The mark of Latin literature in all centuries of the Christian era is artificiality. Petronius stands out among these people like a breath of fresh air. His style is simple, unadorned, and springs from the vitality of spoken Latin. The characters in Petronius speak a Latin which carefully reflects (or betrays) their position in life. Slaves communicate in ungrammatical language, full of colloquialisms, but also full of life. The reader of the *Satyricon* is certain the characters were once alive. Page after page Petronius writes in a way which anyone with a feeling for language can appreciate, especially after coming away from a reading of his contemporaries, Seneca and Lucan. But the naturalness of Petronius' Latin belies his studied style, and its simplicity bears no mark of its polish. Petronius is surely the consummate artist, placing each word in position, choosing that word because it carries the exact shade of meaning needed.

SILVER LATIN LITERATURE

In general all Latin literature of the Empire, or of all centuries A.D., has been termed "Silver Latin." Literature of the Roman Republic is called "Golden Latin," and carries with it the idea that as gold is more precious than silver, so Republican literature is preferable to Empire. This is partially true. The Empire had fewer great writers, but some of its artists like Petronius equaled or surpassed those of the Golden Age.

Ovid (43 B.C.-18 A.D.) Among the most popular works of Ovid are the Art of Love, the Loves, and the Metamorphoses. Ovid's ability to put Latin into verse was second to none; he did not, however, always produce high quality material. He loved life and would have lived it fully, had not the emperor exiled him to the Black Sea for much of it. The erotic held a special fascination for him, and much of his good work concerns the war between the sexes.

Seneca (4 B.C.-65 A.D.) The leading Stoic philosopher of his day, Seneca wrote many tracts on philosophical questions. Among his extant works are nine plays, many letters, and the Apocolocyntosis. Seneca was the tutor of Nero in his early days, and while he remained, Seneca was a good influence over the unbalanced emperor.

Persius (34–62 A.D.) In his short life Persius wrote only six satires with a total of only five hundred lines. A friend of Seneca and Lucan, Persius was also a Stoic. His **satires** are structurally very involved and almost contorted. He satirizes manners of the day.

Lucan (39–65 A.D.) As the nephew of Seneca, Lucan was quickly accepted at the imperial court. His only extant work is an **epic**, the Civil War. Lucan changed the nature of **epic** by dropping its mythological subjects and moving it closer to history. His Civil War is verbose and overdone.

Statius (40–96 A.D.) Refusing to follow the lead of Lucan, Statius returned to old-style **epic** when writing his Thebaid. Though it was very popular in the Middle Ages, the Thebaid is all but forgotten today.

Martial (40–104 A.D.) Epigrams almost begin and end with Martial, whose 1561 short poems cover virtually every subject. From exquisite little poems on the death of a young girl or a biting **satire** on an often-widowed poisoner, Martial can fall all the way to a low level of obscene poetry.

Tacitus (55–117 A.D.) Perhaps the greatest Roman historian, Tacitus described the rise (or fall) of the Empire from the death of Augustus. Writing in a clipped and epigrammatic style, Tacitus longed for a return to Republican Rome.

Juvenal (60–128 A.D.) The name of Juvenal is synonymous with satire. The wife of the emperor, women in general, conditions in Rome, and the futility of life are all subjects for Juvenal. Over the ages Juvenal has had a telling influence on all satirists.

Apuleius (125–190 A.D.) Besides Petronius' *Satyricon*, the only Latin novel to survive from antiquity is Apuleius' *Metamorphoses*, better known as *The Golden Ass*. Apuleius' Latin does not have the charm of Petronius' easy style, but he does tell a good story about Lucius, the man who changes from human to ass and then back again.

FIRST CENTURY ROMAN EMPIRE

The mark of the first-century A.D. Roman Empire is stability, both economic and political. The citizens sacrificed freedom under the Republic to gain a respite from civil war under the Empire. The Emperors that Petronius lived under are known as the Julio-Claudians: Augustus (27 B.C.–14 A.D.); Tiberius (14–37 A.D.); Caligula (37–41 A.D.); Claudius (41–54 A.D.); Nero (54–68 A.D.). Of these Augustus died in bed; Tiberius, it appears, gave himself over to every form of vice, one of which killed him; Caligula went mad, made his horse consul, and finally was mercifully assassinated by the Praetorian Guard; Claudius was poisoned by his last wife, Agrippina; Nero was forced to commit suicide. Through it all, however, these men like good Romans ran the Empire in a business-like fashion. The Empire was generally well governed by an extremely capable civil service and diplomatic corps, and commerce flourished. The average citizen was better off at this time than he had been any time previous. Not until the nineteenth century would the average man on the street have a better material life. There was some sporadic persecution of Christians, but nothing like the persecutions Christians would later inflict on each other or on "pagans." Citizens were safe to travel in the cities, countryside, on the sea, and in foreign countries. Pirates and highwaymen were kept to a minimum by police vigilance, and a system of hotels was set up for travelers. Mail moved more swiftly in Italy under the Julio-Claudians than it does now. The courts protected the poor from the rich, and everybody from government officials. Roman citizens like St. Paul could appeal to the Emperor himself. The city of Rome had fire and police departments, government-sponsored housing, aid to the poor and orphans, running water, a good sewer system, public games and baths, and regular and reasonably priced food supplies. Materially the Empire and its citizens were well cared for. Spiritually the Empire was alive and growing and was a viable force for administering the needs of the entire Mediterranean world.

PETRONIUS IN THE TWENTIETH CENTURY

Heartily admired and often discussed by modern writers, Petronius really "came into his own" in the twentieth century.

Soon after the rediscovery of the "Banquet of Trimalchio" scene in the 1640s, Petronius became a favorite conversation piece among writers of all persuasions. For example, Jeremy Taylor (1613–1667), often called "the Shakespeare of the Pulpit," talks warmly of Petronius as a personality in *The Rule and Exercise of Holy Dying* (1651); Taylor quotes Petronius appreciatively in his other works. Alexander Pope (1688–1744), in *An Essay on Criticism* (1711), includes Petronius among those classical writers worth reading for their critical attitudes toward literature:

> **See Dionysius Homer's thoughts refine, And call new beauties forth from every line! Fancy and art in gay Petronius please, The scholar's learning, with the courtier's ease. In grave Quintilian's copious work, we find The justest rules, and clearest method joined ...**

And when George Gordon, Lord Byron (1788–1824) composed his *English Bards and Scotch Reviewers* (1809), he made good use of both the man Petronius, the "Arbiter of Elegance" of Nero's court, and the writer Petronius, who included literary criticism in his *Satyricon*. Youthful Byron, aiming to ridicule a certain Scottish critic who, in Byron's opinion, was presuming to act as a literary dictator, wrote:

> **Behold the new Petronius of the day,**
> **The Arbiter of pleasure and of play.**

Around the turn of the century, Petronius' popularity increased enormously, probably because modern writers have felt a great kinship with him. His period and ours have much in common; Petronius, like us, lived at the end of one era, at the beginning of another; he too suffered the pangs of uncertainty and transition; like us, he laughed so that he would not weep.

The rebellious Victorian, Oscar Wilde (1856–1900), wit, dramatist, and poet, is credited with a breezy and colloquial translation of Petronius. In Wilde's novel, *The Picture of Dorian Gray* (1891), the main character reflects on the possibility of his becoming the Victorian Petronius. And the great Polish novelist and Nobel Prize winner Henryk Sienkiewicz (1846–1916) used Petronius as one of his main characters in his historical novel about Nero's times, *Quo Vadis?* (*Where are you going?*) Made into a spectacular two-hour film in Italy in 1912, *Quo Vadis?* became a landmark in cinematic history and its title the dominant question for our time.

In a letter to Lady Ottoline Morrell (dated 1 February 1916), the novelist D. H. Lawrence declared that he much preferred Petronius to Dostoevsky. The statement is especially interesting when we remember that both Petronius and Dostoevsky were then emerging into the limelight in the English-speaking world. In *Crome Yellow* (1921), the first novel of Aldous Huxley (1894–1960), the hero actually (and very symbolically) tries to kill himself in exactly the same way that Petronius did!

Petronius really arrived as a symbolic figure for our time when T. S. Eliot (1888–1965) published his *The Waste Land* (1922). Eliot, who had taken a Latin course in Petronius at Harvard, uses several lines from the *Satyricon* (chapter 48) as the superscription for his poem:

The Waste Land:

"Nam Sibyllam quidem Cumis ego ipse oculis meis vidi in ampulla pendere, et cum illi pueri dicerent: respondebat illa:

("Once, with my own eyes, I saw the Sybil at Cumae hanging in a cage, and when the boys said to her, 'Sybil, what do you want?' she replied, 'I want to die.'")

Christopher Fry, English playwright (1907-), based his very successful 1946 play, A Phoenix Too Frequent, on Petronius' tale of the *Widow of Ephesus* (chapters 111–112). In Fry's hands, this famous Petronian material becomes a poetic expression of the triumph of the Life-Force over the Death-Wish.

Petronius also figures prominently in the works of Lawrence Durrell (1912-). Durrell used the "Arbiter of Elegance" as a leading character in his play Acte; there are frequent echoes of and references to Petronius in Durrell's masterpiece, The Alexandria Quartet, especially in *Mountolive* (1959) and in *Clea*

(1960). Durrell and Henry Miller discuss the Roman novelist in their collected letters.

By the late 1960s Petronius had become a major influence and a by-word in many contemporary arts. In 1968 Julian Mitchell, young English writer, published his novel *The Undiscovered Country*, the first large-scale work conceived in its entirety in imitation of the *Satyricon*. In 1969, Federico Fellini, Italian filmmaker, produced a cinematic version called Fellini's *Satyricon*; another Italian, Gian Luigi Polidoro, produced a wide-screen film called simply *Satyricon*; and in the same year the Petronian work was rendered into musical comedy (with a 1920 setting) at the Stratford Festival in Stratford, Ontario.

By 1970, as a consequence of his successful translation into several modern media, Petronius was on everybody's reading list. This enthusiastic revival of interest in an "obscure" ancient writer demonstrates once again that in every age, the avant-garde can find new inspiration, new models, in the Greek and Roman classics. As Professor Paul MacKendrick has said, "To come to know a fragment of our past is to recognize a piece of ourselves."

THE SATYRICON

OVERVIEW

....

To prepare the reader for a detailed commentary on the *Satyricon*, we shall first provide an overall summary of the extant portions of the work; a check-list of characters; and then a discussion of the missing books.

SUMMARY

The extant portion of the *Satyricon* opens with the end of Book 14. Encolpius, the narrator, together with his friend Ascyltus are attending a lecture given by Agamemnon, an itinerant professor of rhetoric. Because they are bored to death with the lecture, both leave and are mistakenly led to a brothel. On returning to their apartment, they quarrel over the affections of Giton and decide to part ways (chapters 1–11). After losing a cloak whose seams were lined with gold pieces, Encolpius apparently recovers it from a farmer with the aid of Ascyltus (chapters 12–15). In a lost portion of the *Satyricon* Encolpius had offended Priapus, a Near-Eastern fertility god; Quartilla, a priestess of Priapus and a lecherous woman of the first rank, has come to seek redress. There follows a real Roman orgy. Priestess, Encolpius, Ascyltus,

Giton, and servants all join in the drinking and debauching. After more than two days of celebrating, the heroes extricate themselves and prepare for Trimalchio's banquet (chapters 16-26). The longest connected narrative in the extant *Satyricon* is "Trimalchio's Banquet" which accounts for about one-third of the 141 chapters (chapters 26-78). The entire banquet revolves around Trimalchio, a former slave but now a slave owner, and a man of considerable means. He owns a large villa around Naples, probably at Puteoli. The guests invited to this feast range from a stone-mason, the guest of honor, to a convicted felon. Course after course of strange food is brought forward to the accompanying explanation of the host. Tales of witches and werewolves are told, and Trimalchio explains to all assembled, whether willing listeners or not, how and why he became wealthy and why he is proud of never having attended school. The reader begins by laughing at Trimalchio and after some time occasionally laughs with him. As the fire department rushes in to put out what they believe to be a fire, Encolpius and his friends escape and flee to their apartment (chapters 26-78). Since both Encolpius and Ascyltus are in love with Giton, it is decided to part company. Giton chooses Ascyltus, and Encolpius is heartbroken (chapters 79-82). A friendship is begun between Encolpius and a slightly mad poet named Eumolpus, only to be strained when Giton returns and there is again a love-triangle (chapters 83-98). Without knowing whose ship they are boarding, Encolpius and company set sail with Lichas and Tryphaena. In a lost section of the *Satyricon*, Encolpius and Giton had outraged both Lichas and Tryphaena, who now try to get revenge. But vengeance is set aside after a mock-battle, and all become friends. Then, off the coast of southern Italy near Croton, the ship is wrecked and Lichas lost (99-115). Our heroes pretend to be very rich in the hope that the inhabitants of Croton will care for them.

Once Eumolpus makes it known that he will leave his vast fortune to those who are kindest to him, gifts and money are heaped on the recently ship-wrecked friends. Encolpius falls in love with Circe, but finds himself impotent, is cured, and becomes impotent again. The *Satyricon* concludes as Eumolpus announces to the people of Croton that only those who consent to eat his dead body will inherit his fortune (116–141).

THE SATYRICON

CHARACTERS IN THE SATYRICON

*Agamemnon: Professor of rhetoric at Puteoli near Naples, who stands convicted of not practicing what he preaches. He claims high moral and ethical goals for education, then abandons them to expediency; advocates the plain style of speech but uses the turgid.

*Ascyltus: Lover and later enemy of Encolpius. There is a strong homosexual bond between Ascyltus and Encolpius which is broken by Giton. Ascyltus is portrayed as completely depraved without any of the introspection or fine sensitivity of Encolpius. Ascyltus' pleasures are all physical.

Carpus: Slave of Trimalchio.

Chrysis: Maid of Circe and lover of Encolpius; low-born woman with high tastes.

Circe: Wealthy would-be mistress of Encolpius at Croton; high-born woman with low tastes.

---

* Denotes a major character

*Encolpius: Impotent anti-hero and narrator of the *Satyricon*. He is strikingly similar to Ascyltus but is more carefully delineated. Though he is a rogue-hero and not above murder, Encolpius has periods of remorse and self-analysis, and seems to know the difference between right and wrong. As narrator, he speaks at times for Petronius and shows good taste in literature and the arts.

*Eumolpus: Would-be poet, friend of Encolpius and Giton. When Ascyltus departs from the scene, Eumolpus takes his place in the love-triangle with Encolpius and Giton. What Agamemnon is to rhetoric, Eumolpus is to poetry. He professes to be a great poet in an ethical tradition going back to Vergil; he is both bad poet and unscrupulous liar.

*Fortunata: Wife of Trimalchio. Born in the lowest rung of society, she moved up to prostitution, saved her money, married Trimalchio, and then helped him become rich. Along the way she acquired no refinement or taste, but did learn the value of money. She is the watch-dog of Trimalchio's fortune as well as of his pederastic affairs with his slaves.

*Giton: Beloved of Encolpius, Ascyltus, and Eumolpus. Like so many handsome young men or boys, Giton is the object of the affection of older men and illustrates well the bisexual nature of at least the intellectual class in the ancient world. He has a true flare for the theatrical.

Gorgias: Legacy-hunter at Croton who agrees to eat Eumolpus' dead body.

———————

*   Denotes a major character

Habinnas: Stone-mason and friend of Trimalchio. His wealth, like that of Trimalchio, is the only thing that makes him important.

Hermerus: Guest of Trimalchio.

Lichas: Ship captain and first enemy, then friend of Encolpius.

Nicerus: Guest of Trimalchio and great raconteur.

*Oenothea: Priestess of Priapus at Croton. As the servant of Priapus, a fertility god, Oenothea like Quartilla is lecherous. Her mind is ever on the erotic; her special realm is curing impotence.

Pannychis: Young maid of Quartilla.

Philomela: Legacy-hunter at Croton.

*Priapus: Fertility god who hounds Encolpius. Though he does not appear in the extant *Satyricon*, his power is felt by many, especially by the impotent Encolpius.

Proselenus: A lecherous faith-healer.

Pschye: Maid of Quartilla.

*Quartilla: Priestess of Priapus and sponsor of the orgy in chapters 16–26. She is a figure drawn without any redeeming feature. Although she is meant to be a temple-prostitute, only a deity like Priapus would claim her for his own.

Scintilla: Wife of Habinnas; a duplicate of Fortunata.

---

* Denotes a major character

*Trimalchio: Wealthy ex-slave and host of the banquet. He is almost without manners or any social graces. When he speaks, he condemns himself as a fool. Because it is only in superficial ways that he tries to put on airs, Trimalchio gains understanding and sympathy from the audience. Outside the very narrow business world of profit and loss, Trimalchio is totally incompetent. He is, through it all, a gentle fool, almost never malicious.

Tryphaena: Prostitute, friend of Giton and Lichas.

---

* Denotes a major character

THE SATYRICON

RECONSTRUCTION OF THE PLOT

....

| MISSING BOOKS

From the manuscripts of the *Satyricon*, we can infer that the extant portion begins late in Book 14. Not only is much lost, but also much of what remains is fragmentary. Therefore, some of the reconstruction and interpretation is open to discussion. It appears that the action of the full-length *Satyricon* began at Massilia, modern Marseilles, in southern France, where some kind of plague had settled on the city. Encolpius, though convicted of impersonating the ithyphallic god Priapus, was allowed to go free on condition that he first serve as a ritual scape-goat to rid the city of its ills. He was maintained at public expense for one year; then the city priests in a magic rite transferred the plague or whatever trouble it had to Encolpius, forbidding him to return to Massilia. This ritual was not uncommon in antiquity; its efficacy is doubtful. Somewhere, perhaps during the trip from Massilia to Naples, Encolpius met Giton and Ascyltus.

LOST EPISODES

There are five lost **episodes** referred to in the extant *Satyricon*, which must have occurred in the early, missing portions. (1) Encolpius and Ascyltus robbed the villa of Lycurgus and killed its owner. The money stolen at this time is lost but recovered in chapters 12–15. (2) Encolpius was apparently condemned for some crime to fight in the arena; see Chapter 9. (3) By his own confession in a letter to Circe in chapter 130, Encolpius admits to murder and robbing a temple. (4) In another lost episode around Naples, Encolpius seduced Hydele, the wife of Lichas, and made Tryphaena the main subject in a public scandal. But Lichas and Tryphaena get their revenge in chapters 99–115. (5) In some way or other at the secret rites of Priapus, which were overseen by Quartilla, Encolpius committed some foul act, but escaped. Quartilla wins her revenge for this desecration in chapters 16–26.

THE SATYRICON

DETAILED ANALYSIS

PROFESSOR AGAMEMNON (CHAPTERS 1–5)

Story

Encolpius and Ascyltus are attending a lecture by a local, well-known professor, Agamemnon. The lesson for the day concerns education in general and the sad state to which it has sunk: what students are taught in school has nothing to do with reality. Encolpius complains bitterly:

> I think schools produce only fools. The reason is that students are not taught relevant material. How can they learn about reality when they are forced to write practice speeches about pirates in chains standing on the shore, or tyrants writing orders to sons to decapitate their fathers, or oracles demanding that two or three virgins be sacrificed? Do you call that education? Why, a dishwasher in a greasy kitchen has a better chance of becoming a gourmet cook than our students do of becoming educated in modern schools.

Encolpius goes on to complain that it is the study of rhetoric (that is, science of speaking: theory, voice control, persuasion, etc.) that ruins education, and that the great artists of early Greece and Rome were taught to speak and write in a plain style. Now everything sounds as though a lawyer wrote it, and, in fact, only other lawyers can understand it. The influence of contemporary rhetoric as taught in schools makes both oratory and literature artificial, verbose, overblown, and ugly.

Agamemnon, who makes his living by teaching rhetoric, tries to smooth over a bad situation:

> **Professors do share a part of the blame for this. But unless we tell students what they want to hear, they will not pay their tuition…I think the parents of the students are to blame. They want their immature children to be finished products immediately, to go out into the world and make vast sums of money, to say they went to college, and to be famous.**

For his concluding remarks, he delivers a 22-line impromptu poem on education and relates how much better it was in the good-old-days when students studied good-old-subjects.

Comment

The question of the best type of education was ever on the mind of intellectual Romans. During the Republic the study of rhetoric was a valuable asset to any young man interested in law, politics, or education. Even those not born in the patrician order like Cicero could, by becoming outstanding rhetoricians, still rise to great heights. Even generals and business men were expected to speak well. Familiarity with formal rhetoric was also imperative for those who wished to move up socially or to keep a high social position. Rhetoric quickly took control of school curricula and replaced all other subjects which were not immediately relevant. But when Rome fell under an Emperor, the need for ambitious politicians and lawyers fell to zero. The Emperor and his bureaucratic administration tended to all affairs of law and government. Though rhetoric became an empty and artificial study because it had lost its basic reason for existence, it retained a terrible hold on education, supplanting all other studies, and grew further and further apart from reality. Encolpius condemns not only the irrelevance of rhetoric but goes on to berate the pompous and verbose kind of rhetoric called Asianic style. The best style, Encolpius contends, is Attic, which is a pure and simple **exposition**, stressing naturalness. As far as can be ascertained, Petronius himself preferred the Attic style, and in chapters 1–5 Encolpius thus speaks for Petronius.

FROM BROTHEL TO BROTHER (CHAPTERS 6–11)

Story

With the discussion of rhetoric becoming a bore, Ascyltus flees the lecture hall with Encolpius not far behind. Both young men are unfamiliar with the city; they are led via different routes to the same low-class brothel. Encolpius finds his way into the brothel with the help of an old hag, but Ascyltus has been solicited by a perverted aristocrat. The text of the *Satyricon* is fragmentary at this point. When the story continues, we find Giton in tears lying on a bed in the apartment and Encolpius attending him. Giton cries to Encolpius:

> **Your brother, or is it friend, Ascyltus, was here in this room a short while ago and tried to take me by force.**

When I shouted for help, he drew his sword and said, "If you are Lucretia, you have found your Tarquin."

Encolpius turns on Ascyltus and condemns him with the strongest abuse, only to find himself attacked by Ascyltus:

You filthy gladiator. You are reproaching me? Everyone here knows you escaped from the arena, and that even on your best day you could not handle a decent woman. I played the role of your brother in the garden, and now I see you have a new brother in this apartment.

Encolpius changes the subject of discussion back to Agamemnon, and both break out in laughter over the funny old professor. Ascyltus and Encolpius admit to each other that the presence of both makes an intolerable love-triangle and one must go. They agree to divide all possessions, and Ascyltus consents to move to another apartment. After a break in the text, the action resumes as Ascyltus surprises Encolpius and Giton making love, picks up a strap, and begins to whip Encolpius. Again the text breaks off.

Comment

It is important to recognize at the outset the homosexual relationships among Encolpius, Ascyltus, and Giton. The term "brother" is regularly employed in the Latin to indicate this relationship. Homosexuality was an accepted custom in antiquity and practiced in the best circles. Perhaps, instead of homosexuality it is better to speak of bisexuality, because many sophisticated ancients chose partners from both the opposite sex and the same sex. From our vantage point in the twentieth century, and after thorough indoctrination in Judaeo-Christian ethics, we find ourselves somewhat uneasy when confronted with homosexuality. Not so the Greeks and Romans.

The story of Encolpius' mistaking a brothel for his house is one of many humorous **episodes** in the novel; it reflects in general on Roman society where prostitution was such a thriving business that the state taxed it. When Ascyltus says to Giton, "If you are Lucretia, you have found your Tarquin," he recalls a bit of Roman history when kings still ruled Rome: the king's son, Tarquin, raped Lucretia, thereby encouraging revolt. In this section Ascyltus mentions Encolpius' escape from the arena to which he had been condemned. Criminals convicted of certain heinous crimes were sentenced to the gladiatorial arena. There is really no way to determine Encolpius' crime.

THE STOLEN CLOAK (CHAPTERS 12–15)

Story. After a missing section of the text, the story continues with Encolpius, Ascyltus, and Giton entering the forum of a city near Naples. They have come at night to sell a stolen cloak to an unsuspecting customer, but suddenly they recognize the farmer who found a rag-coat containing their gold coins. The gold coins, sewn into the seams of the rag-coat, had not been discovered by the farmer. And the stolen cloak which Encolpius hopes to sell is really the property of the farmer! Both sides recognize their own property and cry, "Thief:" one wants gold, the other his cloak. Ambulance-chasing lawyers are quickly at the scene of the dispute, demanding to take possession of the evidence. The argument is resolved, and both sides retrieve their own goods. Stolen property cases cannot be resolved in courts full of bribes, claims Ascyltus, and recites a short poem about the power of money and the weakness of the law:

Law has no sting where money is king;
Privation breeds fools where money rules,
And vows of poverty yield to cash.
Truly justice is blind and courts unkind,
Where causes are lost for the price of the cost,
Unless the judge is bribed with more cash.

Comment

While there is no way of knowing how Encolpius stole the cloak, a suggestion can be offered about the provenance of the gold coins. This could be part of the plunder obtained from the murder of Lycurgus and rape of his villa, mentioned in chapter 117. Encolpius is set to take the case of the gold coins to court, but Ascyltus reminds him of the corruption in the courts, where the largest bribe carries the day. Petronius' charge against Roman legal procedure is strong, but is also supported by evidence from Juvenal and Martial. Apparently this **episode** is a true reflection of contemporary social conditions.

PRIAPUS AND HIS PRIESTESS (CHAPTERS 16-26)

Story. As was mentioned earlier, in a lost portion of the *Satyricon* Encolpius in some way profaned the secret rites of Priapus. The most prominent feature of Priapus is the phallus; his usual representations in statue form show him to be nothing more than a phallus with certain man-like attributes. Priapus was a fertility god, thought to bring good luck. Most frequently his statues appear in gardens or in fields where at times they are used as scarecrows. The Romans never worshipped Priapus as a deity, but it is sure that his generative powers were held in awe. Rather than an object of veneration, Priapus must be considered an object of humor and mirth, evoking a broad grin with slightly obscene attitudes.

Divine retribution comes to Encolpius in the form of Quartilla, priestess of Priapus and a lecherous woman, portrayed by Petronius to be one in a long line of evil women. Encolpius, Ascyltus, and Giton have just finished supper when they hear a rap on the door. Their immediate terror at the thought of a visitor is heightened when the door falls off its hinge and admits Quartilla and her maids. The older maid of Quartilla wastes no time in accusing Encolpius of having offended Priapus by disturbing his rites. Our heroes have no chance to react before Quartilla falls on the bed and is convulsed in tears. Once her composure is found, Quartilla speaks:

> **How could you dare to do it? These acts of yours were more audacious than those of Heracles. By god, I pity you. You do not spy on secret rites and get away with it! This whole area is so full of deities that it is easier to meet a god than a man. But I am not here for vengeance. It is just that I pity you; you are so young to have committed such a serious crime. On the very night of your offense a terrible chill hit me, and I now fear that I have become frigid.**

Quartilla goes on to warn Encolpius and company that they must never disclose the rites they had observed. Before entering, Quartilla had ordered her servants to seal off the hotel and admit no men, so that she could have peace during her frigidity "treatments." The *Satyricon* at this point becomes extremely fragmentary, but the following scenes can be isolated: there is a general orgy of the first order; Encolpius, Ascyltus, and Giton are bound head and feet and sexually assaulted. Quartilla prepares a huge feast for our heroes and invites all her attendants and slaves. We are told that the party will last three days. Some of the slaves try to steal the sterling flatware but are forced to abandon their plans when they cannot agree on who should get what. This whole **episode** concludes with a mock-marriage between Giton, aged 12 or so, and Pannychis, aged 7. While the marriage is in the process of consummation, Quartilla finds a chink in the bedroom door and watches the ceremony.

| Comment

The *Satyricon* is in a way a **parody** of the *Odyssey*. Poseidon hounded Odysseus over land and sea, and Petronius has Priapus pursue Encolpius. But where Poseidon was one of the great Olympian gods, Priapus is more or less a joke. Thus the **parody**. This all-night ritual is called a pervigilium in Latin; Pannychis, who is the object of the barbaric ritual at the conclusion of chapters 16–26, means all-night. Even in outrageous scenes Petronius cannot keep from making little jokes or puns. Because of Encolpius' offense against him, Priapus had made Quartilla, his priestess, frigid. To rectify the situation Quartilla comes to Encolpius, but Encolpius, because of the same offense, has himself become impotent. Quartilla then arranges the horrible ritual, whereby Pannychis is deflowered, in hope that by observing it Quartilla might regain her old strength. In his book *The City of God* (Book 6, chapter 9) St. Augustine condemns this very ritual of Priapus. Because of the fragmentary state of the Satyricon at this point, there is no way of knowing how the **episode** ends.

DINNER WITH TRIMALCHIO (CHAPTERS 26–78)

Story

The Host Arrives (26–33). Encolpius, Ascyltus, and Giton arrive at the home of Trimalchio, who is discovered playing ball with his slaves. The game stops, Trimalchio calls for a chamber pot to be brought to the field, urinates, washes his hands, and then dries them in his slave's hair. This is the introduction to Trimalchio. The wealth of Trimalchio is displayed everywhere with ostentation: he dresses like a king in purple robes; grotesque and gilded paintings depict stories from his life; a retinue of slaves follows him everywhere indoors and out; everywhere the walls are full of inane inscriptions:

> **Beware of the dog**
> **30–31 December the Master dines out**

All the guests are seated, but the order is mixed-up and Trimalchio ignores the best etiquette. As the hors d'oeuvre are served, Trimalchio is carried into the sound of music; his appearance is so comical that Encolpius almost breaks out in laughter. Every piece of silver has Trimalchio's name on it and the weight of silver in it. His opening remarks to his guests are unbelievable:

> **Dear friends, it is not really convenient for me to eat this early. But I do it for you. I postponed certain little conveniences because of you. Now, pardon me as I finish my ball game.**

The guests are meanwhile served eggs for which Trimalchio apologizes as they may be "ripe." Encolpius is about to throw his egg away and his breakfast up, when he discovers that the eggs are stuffed.

Comment

Trimalchio belongs to the class of nouveau riche which grew very large in the prosperity of the first century. Though he has vast stores of money and acres of property, Trimalchio lacks education, the rudiments of etiquette, and most importantly, taste. Almost ninety different foods will be served before the banquet is over: most are so common and cheap as to be available even to the poor. His lack of table manners is rivaled only by his lack of education. His guests, like his friends, are from the bottom rung of society, former slaves, ex-convicts, and escaped convicts. Among such people it is difficult for Trimalchio not to excel.

Story

A Roman Feast (34–41). Trimalchio returns to the table and offers everyone more wine. After ordering that a silver dish dropped by a slave be swept up with the rubbish, the host points out that because slaves stink so much he has placed the guests where they need not come into contact with them. As Falernian wine, guaranteed to be 100 years old, is set out, Trimalchio becomes maudlin, orders his favorite skeleton to be produced, and then recites a terrible poem on the frailty of life. Trimalchio says:

> **Gentlemen, this stuff was bottled more than 100 years ago. Why yesterday, I served cheap booze, and the guests were much more distinguished than you.**

The next course is brought out on a tray made to hold the twelve signs of the zodiac. The cook has placed an appropriate food over each sign. For Trimalchio the opportunity is golden:

> I will explain the zodiac for you. This is heaven, house of the twelve gods, and it turns into the twelve signs. At one time it turns into Aries the Ram. Whoever is born here has lots of wool and sheep, a hard head, a forehead like brass, and stiff horns. People with head problems like professors and morons are born under Aries.

And so it goes through the entire zodiac. For carving meat, Trimalchio has a servant named Carver. With the terrible pun, "Carver, carve'er," he is ordered to work. One of the guests at the table tells Encolpius about Trimalchio's earlier life. His wife is named Fortunata, a hard woman who rose from prostitution to run his estates. And his estates are very large, stretching all over Italy (so he says) and producing every kind of edible delicacy. Furthermore, Encolpius is warned not to despise Trimalchio's friends. Even though they once were slaves, it is inadvisable to look down on them. To the sound of music and singing, a regular feature at Trimalchio's, a huge sow is carried in. When it is gutted, thrushes fly out; they are caught and passed out to the guests.

Comment

Every dish served by Trimalchio is disguised as something else. Like a child he loves fun and games. Nor can he let well-enough be. Each new dish, each topic of discussion is explained ad nauseam by Trimalchio. Never realizing his mistakes, he believes himself equal to anyone or anything. His wealth gives him confidence, and his power of life-and-death over slaves and friends keeps him from being contradicted or mocked. Friends and notables are entertained at Trimalchio's house frequently, so that he might get the opportunity to display his wealth, cleverness, and greatness of mind. Through it all he remains a lovable fraud.

> **Story**

The Guests Alone (42–46). Because of bladder troubles Trimalchio leaves the dining room. With the host gone, the guests relax and talk of everything from politics to drink. Seleucus, fresh from the funeral of a friend, remarks about the futility of life: men are like flies and bubbles, exposed on every side to danger; the doctors killed poor Chrysanthus with their crazy diets; even his wife showed no emotion; loving your wife is a waste of good energy. Another guest interrupts and says that Chrysanthus has lived well enough and made a good deal of money. After further discussion of him, Ganymedes breaks in and changes the subject to local politics, rising prices, and the good-old-days:

> **Back some years ago things were different. People had religion. Women would put on their Sunday clothes, climb the hill to the temple and pray for rain. And, by God, it would rain. They would come down that hill looking like drowned rats. Now we have a drought. No religion, no rain.**

Echion, a ragseller, wants to talk about more pleasant things like Glyco's catching his wife in bed with a servant and then condemning the servant to the arena. And Mammaea is going to pay for a feast for the whole city. Echion tries to coax Agamemnon to visit his villa. The food will be good and his sons would like to see Agamemnon since one day they will be his pupils. Education, says Echion, is money in the bank, and a trade cannot be stolen by thieves.

> **Comment**

Table talk from Roman times to the present has not changed much. The *Satyricon* is a valuable social document of the times because it is one of the few records to preserve the conversations and thoughts of everyday people. While Trimalchio is present, he completely dominates the conversation, hitting in everywhere. After he departs, the guests discuss topics important to them. From their conversation we learn a good deal about Trimalchio's friends, most of whom are wealthy, were once slaves like Trimalchio, and rose to great wealth but never to high social station. In this section Petronius delivers one of his most sarcastic remarks about old Roman religion.

Story

An Elegant Table (47–53). Trimalchio returns to the table and explains that his constipation forced him to leave. Any guest with similar problems is told that he will be excused if he is forced to pass gas at the table. Trimalchio adds that those who try to contain themselves could die if the trapped gases rise to their brains. Encolpius buries his face in his winecup to keep from laughing. Three white pigs are led in; Trimalchio orders that the oldest be killed and prepared whole. Turning to his guests he says:

> **I never buy food or wine; everything at my banquets comes from my estates. My vineyard extends from Tarracina to Tarentum, and I would like to add Sicily to my lands, so that when I feel like going to Africa I never have to leave my own lands.**

After debating with Agamemnon on several points and confusing and mixing-up well-known Greek myths, Trimalchio turns his attention to the large pig which has just been brought in. On close inspection he discovers that the pig has been prepared without first being gutted. The cook is ordered to be whipped, but the guests plead for his safety. Trimalchio agrees, if the cook guts the pig immediately. As he cuts it open, sausages and pudding roll out. As a reward the cook is given a dish of Corinthian bronze, whose origin Trimalchio is quick to relate:

> **People always ask me how it is that I am the only one who owns genuine Corinthian dishes. It is really quite simple: I buy all of my bronze ware from a man named Corinth. I am no fool though; I know the origin of all Corinthian bronze. After Hannibal had captured Troy, that sneaky devil piled all the bronze, silver, and gold statues in a heap and melted them into a bronze alloy. From this, artisans made objects of every kind.**

Trimalchio tells his guests also about a large silver bowl he owns which shows Cassandra killing her sons, and another bowl portraying Daedalus shutting Niobe in the Trojan horse. Trimalchio, who is now very drunk, is about to perform a dance in the dining room when Fortunata stops him. The whole banquet is interrupted by an accountant who reads aloud the business report of Trimalchio's estate for 26 July. He is replaced by a troupe of acrobats who, Trimalchio confesses, he prefers to all other artists: horn-players and acrobats are the only real, artistic professionals.

| Comment

Trimalchio's discussion at the table of his constipation problems is one of the high points of Petronian humor. The freedom offered by the host to defecate and pass gas in the dining room is believed to be a sign of taste. The guests are forced to hide their laughter in their cups. Trimalchio's boast that his lands extend from Tarracina to Tarentum is nonsense: it is a distance of some 200 miles. Only a drunk man like Trimalchio could then add that he hopes to buy Sicily. The **episode** of the ungutted pig was planned by Trimalchio, who loves surprises and the presentation of one food in the form of another. His story of Corinthian bronze is sheer imagination or, at best, utter confusion. Hannibal never conquered Troy and, in fact, lived a thousand years later. Trimalchio's confusion of well-known myths is so bad it becomes funny: Cassandra had no children; she was Priam's daughter and after fall of Troy became Agamemnon's mistress. Daedalus and Niobe had nothing whatsoever to do with the Trojan horse. Trimalchio remains the center of attraction at the banquet, while the guests compliment him and set the stage for his movements. Though it is agreed by all that Trimalchio is a buffoon, he has some redeeming traits. Because he rose from the low position of slavery, there is a never-ending attempt on his part to move in higher society and to express himself on matters of taste. Money, he believes, will cure all ills. Of all those in the *Satyricon*, he is the only major character who can be described as non-malicious. No matter the situation, he seems to be able to adjust to it and quite often to enjoy it.

Story

Elegant Guests (56–40). A slave suddenly stumbles and falls on Trimalchio reclining at the table. Doctors rush toward him but Encolpius suspects a trick, especially when a slave is beaten for using white bandages instead of purple, the royal color and favorite of Trimalchio. With great fanfare, Trimalchio frees the slave who fell on him so that it cannot be said that he was hurt by a slave. After a discussion and recitation of poetry, Trimalchio speaks about the difficulty of certain professions and extends it even to the difficult tasks of animals. He informs his guests that contrary to what they may have heard, bees vomit honey. Next, small gifts are distributed to the guests. Ascyltus thinks the whole situation is extremely funny and through his laughter implies that the guests are low-class boors. Hermerus, incensed, begins to call Ascyltus names and at the same time to defend himself against the stigma of being a nobody and an uneducated ex-slave:

> **I got some land and the wife has some silver. Twenty mouths and a dog depend on my bringing home the bacon. Then I bought my old lady's freedom so that everybody would keep his hands off her. Laid out four thousand cash for my own freedom.**

Nor does Hermerus spare Giton and Encolpius, but accuses them all of being worthless dandies. Enough is enough and Trimalchio breaks in. He calls upon several reciters to sing parts from Homer and provides a running commentary to their song. But his knowledge of mythology has not improved, and events from Homer are hopelessly confused. Suddenly the ceiling of the dining room opens and small gifts are let down to the guests. Meanwhile the table is refilled with other food, and a slave carries around a bust of Trimalchio for everyone to kiss.

Comment

Trimalchio loves to disguise one food as another, and does so frequently. The whole meal is planned beforehand, and all the slaves act on cue: now they sing, now they feign an accident and fall over him, now they open the sky-light roof. Trimalchio continues to tell stories from mythology and also to confuse the characters and actions so thoroughly that the resulting story is often humorous. This is a tribute to Petronius the artist.

Hermerus' attack on Ascyltus is self-revealing and discloses the evidence of his rise from poverty to riches. It is a socially important disclosure because it illustrates both the conditions and the thinking of the Neronian Age middle class. Morally and intellectually the middle class as portrayed by Petronius is reactionary; in business matters and government spending they appear to be socialists. The final **episode** in this section, when the guests are asked to kiss Trimalchio's bust, shows a rather bewildered host who wants nothing more from his guests than to be loved and admired.

Story

The Final Course is not Dessert (61–78). Nicerus opens this section with one of the finest werewolf stories in any literature. A soldier friend becomes a werewolf while walking through a cemetery. As he attacks a herd of sheep owned by Nicerus' mistress, he is pierced by a spear in the neck. He recovers from his wound after returning to human form, but Nicerus could not associate with him any longer. Trimalchio, not to be outdone, tells a similar story about witches and vampires. The guests, who are superstitious in a simple-folk way, offer prayers for safety from such evils. Many new foods continue to be served. Trimalchio's boy-love Croesus appears with his dog and takes a seat next to the master, as Habinnas and his wife Scintilla enter the banquet. They have just come from another feast. The men and their wives are old friends; all began poor but now are wealthy. After comparing jewelry for a time, the wives turn their attention to their husbands. Trimalchio is doting on Croesus, his misshapen boy-love, and Habinnas on Massa. These young boys are the objects of their masters' affection, and are resented openly and hated inwardly by the wives. After a call for more wine, dessert is brought in and sawdust sprinkled with saffron and vermilion is scattered over the floor. The wives are becoming extremely agitated over the open affection shown by their husbands for the slave boys. The cook continues to send in new courses: one group appears in the forms of various fowl, but all turn out to be made of pork. Another set of slaves appears and pours perfume on the guests and a little in the wine. Trimalchio next invites the slaves to recline with guests, and announces that he will free many of his slaves in his will. Then he orders his will to be read, and gives elaborate instructions to Habinnas, a stonemason, who is at work on Trimalchio's tomb. Trimalchio is obsessed with the idea of death, especially his own, for which he has just now composed this epitaph:

Here Lies
Gaius Pompeius Trimalchio
Maecenatianus
Member Of The Priesthood Of Augustus
He Declined Honors In Rome
Kind Virtuous True
Self - Made
Bequeathed 30,000,000
Never Attended College
Farewell

Trimalchio adjourns the banquet to the baths, and Encolpius and friends try to use this opportunity to escape from the sickening events of the evening. When they find no avenue of escape, because a watch dog will not let them exit, they join in the bath. As a new shift of slaves enters, Trimalchio sees another boy-love of his and begins kissing him. Fortunata is outraged, calls him a dog and promptly receives a glass in the face. Marital bliss is at an end. Trimalchio orders Habinnas to remove Fortunata's name from his tomb, and calms his guests by retelling how he became so wealthy. As a slave he was the boy-love of his master and tumbled the master's wife often. Sentimentality hits a new low when Stichus, a slave, is ordered to carry in Trimalchio's coffin. The old man climbs in and tells his guests: "Pretend I am dead." A funeral trumpeter enters with a blast so loud it attracts the fire brigade, who believe it to be a fire signal. As the firemen begin to break up the house, Encolpius and his friends escape.

Comment

It was an established practice in antiquity that writers of long narrative like Petronius pause at certain points and interrupt their story by inserting short tales. The *Odyssey* and the *Aeneid* illustrate this nicely as does Apuleius in the *Golden Ass* with the "Cupid and Psyche" story. These tales, called frame-narratives or interpolated tales, slow down the action of a story, break its monotony, and give the audience a chance to breathe, before they get more of the same. The werewolf tale is a brief recess in an unending story of food. Trimalchio's obsession with death and the uselessness of life reflects a popular and cynical philosophy of fatal determinism, a belief that man is a mere plaything of the deities. Homosexual relationships again come out into the open, betraying not only Petronius' proclivities but also the open acceptance and established practice of bisexuality in the classical world. In the incident in which Trimalchio invites the slaves to sit with the guests, he betrays his real feeling for them. Trimalchio had spent many years in slavery and had developed a personal philosophy that all men are brothers. This attitude helps to explain the warmth that is attached to the character of Trimalchio.

EUMOLPUS, MAD POET (CHAPTERS 79–90)

Story

Encolpius, Ascyltus, and Giton arrive home dead tired and quickly retire, but Ascyltus steals Giton from Encolpius' bed. Only in the morning does Encolpius discover the evil deed. Ascyltus claims that the only way both can have part of Giton is to split him down the middle with a sword. It is agreed to let Giton choose his partner, and without hesitation he chooses Ascyltus. Encolpius is crushed, and only after some time does he regain the strength to put on his sword and follow Giton. But a burly soldier quickly strips Encolpius of his sword and forces him to give up the pursuit. At this juncture (chapter 81) Encolpius gives a history of his perverted childhood. To entertain himself, Encolpius visits an art gallery where he meets a white-haired old poet named Eumolpus. The conversation is dominated by Eumolpus who decries the low state of poetry and the poverty of poets, especially his own. Eumolpus relates a story (interpolated tale) to Encolpius about his teaching career in Pergamum in Asia Minor. It is a highly entertaining narrative of his seduction of a boy entrusted to his charge for educating. Eumolpus' call for a return to "finer things" and higher morality is perhaps totally vitiated by his unseemly conduct and lack of ethical posture. On seeing a painting of the fall of Troy, Eumolpus produces 65 extemporaneous lines on the subject and is promptly stoned by those around him. Encolpius informs Eumolpus that he will not associate with him if he continues to recite poetry. In fact, Encolpius fills his pockets with stones so that should Eumolpus turn again to recitation, he will be prepared.

Comment

It comes as quite a shock to Encolpius when Giton chooses Ascyltus as his partner. But always lurking in the background is Encolpius' impotence, a lingering malady with which Priapus afflicts him. Eumolpus, Encolpius' new friend, comments on many aspects of good and bad art and literature. While it seems that much of what he says is consistent with Petronian practice, Eumolpus' low repute and lack of ethics and at times lack of taste go a long way toward negating his positive remarks. Poetasters abounded at the time, and many school children had ambitions of becoming great poets. Eumolpus' attempt at poetry here is worthy of the stoning he receives. Frequently Eumolpus bemoans the low state to which all the arts have fallen, the state of poverty in which real artists find themselves, and the recognition accorded to mediocre artists. This same complaint is heard in twentieth-century America and has been voiced in almost every age. Petronius surely does not feel that literature of his own day is inferior to that of earlier generations. A better interpretation seems to be that he finds in such discussions good material for his *Satyricon*. The subject of the theories of art was topical in imperial Rome and was therefore relevant to Petronius' production of realistic literature. Petronius is a literary opportunist and uses certain kinds of material, not because he is emotionally involved in it, but because he can make better use of it than he could of a different type. Then too, the condemnation of a successful person, whether poet or politician, is the most hackneyed of topics. And Eumolpus is the most hackneyed of poets.

NEW LOVE-TRIANGLE (CHAPTERS 91–99)

Story

In the public baths Encolpius finds Giton and, since Eumolpus is again reciting poetry, deserts him. After Giton has explained his reasons for choosing Ascyltus over Encolpius, Eumolpus returns, complaining that the bathers had expelled him for reciting his poetry. From the actions of Eumolpus with Giton,

Encolpius realizes that he has another rival in Eumolpus. Eumolpus relates that he saw Ascyltus, now befriended by a wealthy homosexual. When Eumolpus steals Giton and locks Encolpius in the apartment, Encolpius attempts suicide but stops as Giton returns and threatens his own suicide. When the landlord arrives to investigate the disturbance, Eumolpus quarrels with him in the hall and is quickly trapped there as Encolpius, in an act of revenge, locks him out. The next visitor to the apartment is Ascyltus, now in the service of the wealthy knight, who is offering 1000 sesterces for the return of Giton. He searches Encolpius' apartment but does not discover Giton. Like Odysseus under a sheep, Giton escapes notice by hiding under the bed in the mattress. Eumolpus, however, indignant because he had been locked out, threatens to hand Giton over to Ascyltus but is dissuaded from so doing. After a missing portion in the text, the three adventurers board a ship late at night, and Encolpius promises not to become jealous of Eumolpus and Giton.

Comment

Removal of Ascyltus from the scene allows Encolpius a free hand with Giton. Such freedom is short-lived because of the arrival of Eumolpus, who will be the third partner in this new love-triangle. Petronius continues to portray Eumolpus as a "mad" poet, rejected by all his listeners. Eumolpus believes himself a man of high poetic ability and sound moral principles, but Petronius allows him to contradict both assumptions by his own actions. The **episodes** at the door, where first one and then the other are locked out, are rich in humor and seem accurately to show the neurotic state of the characters who can move in one instant from love to hate and from life to suicide. The incident of Giton hiding under the bed is surely a **parody** of Odysseus' escape from the Cyclops' cave in the *Odyssey* Book 9.

CAPTURE, SHIPWRECK, MORE POETRY (CHAPTERS 100–124)

Story

Only after the ship has set sail do Encolpius and Giton realize that it is operated by Lichas and Tryphaena, feared enemies. In a lost section of the *Satyricon* Encolpius had seduced Hydele, the wife of Lichas, and brought a public scandal down on the head of Tryphaena. After much debate Eumolpus tries to disguise the identity of Encolpius and Giton by painting fake brands on their foreheads. Lichas nevertheless learns of their presence on board and orders them flogged. Tryphaena and her maids run to the rescue as they hear Giton and Encolpius scream, and force Lichas to stop the whippings. A rather bloodless battle erupts and does not cease until Giton pretends to emasculate himself. Peace terms are agreed upon, and a banquet is ordered prepared for the guests on the ship in celebration of that peace. At this point (chapters 111–112) Eumolpus narrates one of the most delightful stories (interpolated narrative) preserved from antiquity: A chaste and virtuous woman of Ephesus was so distressed by her husband's death that she decided to die in the underground vault tomb with him. A Roman soldier, who was ordered to guard three crucified criminals so that their relatives would not remove the bodies, saw a light burning in the underground tomb and proceeded to investigate. He was so taken by the scene of the woman in the tomb that he determined to save her. After preliminary matters had been disposed of, the two fell in love in the tomb; meanwhile the absence of a guard on duty gave the relatives of one of the criminals the opportunity to steal his body. When the soldier saw what had happened, he would have killed himself if the widow had not stopped him. Refusing to lose both her husband and her lover, she helped the soldier lift her husband's body to the cross. After this story has been told, the ship is hit by a storm and wrecked, and Lichas is killed.

Even though the ship is sinking, Eumolpus remains below writing poetry and is removed from the hold only by force. Once on shore the three adventurers turn inland, and, having learned that Croton is nearby, head in that direction. With nothing to do on the long walk, Eumolpus lectures Encolpius on the theories of poetry, and in support of his own beliefs delivers an abbreviated **epic** of 295 lines. Eumolpus claims that too many rhetoricians, tired of law, have turned to poetry. These men bring no inspiration or background to poetry except the study of rhetoric, and many elements of rhetoric are harmful to the writing of poetry.

Comment

The **episode** in which Lichas and Tryphaena first met Encolpius is missing, but its barest outline can be uncovered: Encolpius had outraged both and then escaped. The battle scene on ship and the mock suicide point up the main characters' love for theatrics. Petronius had earlier introduced roles for Lichas and Tryphaena that he might use them here. It is a form of dramatic **irony** employed frequently in episodic narratives to cut down on the total number of actors and also to add an element of cause and effect. Because Lichas had earlier been offended, a kind of retribution is set up by Petronius to serve as a resolution of the **episode**. This episode thus acquires a type of suspense; the reader is led to expect a reaction for every action. Stories like the one about the widow of Ephesus, which stress the idea that things and people are not what they seem to be, are favorites of Petronius: characters such as Eumolpus who preach morality, turn out to be the most immoral. Eumolpus' theories of literature (chapter 118) appear to be consistent with those of Petronius, but because he is such a disreputable character one can never be sure how Petronius means for us to understand them.

The widow of Ephesus story was adapted by Christopher Fry in his successful verse-play entitled *A Phoenix Too Frequent*. Petronius apparently composed the short **epic** and placed it in the mouth of Eumolpus to counter the new-style **epic** of Lucan. In his epic the Civil War Lucan altered the accepted style of earlier **epic**: he dropped all mythological **themes** and characters and removed the divine machinery (**deus ex machina**). For his subject Lucan chose the Civil War of 48 B. C. between Caesar and Pompey. This was a radical departure from the **epic** of Vergil, and Petronius, a literary conservative, calls for a return to Vergilian **epic**. He writes these 295 lines to show Lucan, as it were, how **epic** ought to be composed.

CIRCE THE SORCERESS (CHAPTERS 125-141)

Story

After learning from a stranger on the road that only two types of people inhabit Croton, those with legacies to leave and those seeking legacies, Eumolpus develops a plan to defraud the legacy-hunters. Giton and Encolpius are to act as the slaves of Eumolpus, a wealthy land-owner from North Africa whose ship was wrecked in the sea off Croton. At the present time he has no funds, but is expecting millions from Africa momentarily. To whet the appetite of the legacy-hunters, Eumolpus pretends he is dying of consumption and preparing his will. The legacy-hunters are totally deceived and move Eumolpus and slaves to a palatial estate where everything is provided. Meanwhile Encolpius is approached by Chrysis, a maid of Circe, on behalf of Circe to learn whether or not he would accept Circe as a lover. It seems that Circe, a noble lady, prefers slaves and gladiators to men of her own station. Circe and Encolpius, who is living under the assumed name Polyaenus, meet in a garden and almost immediately embrace. Circe is aware of his affair with Giton, and since Encolpius is impotent with her, Circe is outraged. She sends him a sarcastic letter telling him to contract an undertaker, because anyone with his type paralysis would shortly die. Encolpius writes back that he will do better next time. Circe sends a witch named Proselenus to cure him and she effects at least a momentary cure. But in their next encounter, Encolpius again cannot satisfy Circe. This time, however, she sends not a letter but servants to beat him. Encolpius is at the edge of total despair and resorts even to writing poems against his offending member. Circe sends another witch named Oenothea to heal Encolpius, and both Proselenus and Oenothea work over him. They are more interested, however, in their own sexual desires than in curing their patient, and Encolpius barely escapes with his life. The text becomes fragmentary, but from what remains it seems that Encolpius is finally cured of his impotence and Chrysis falls in love with him. Meanwhile Eumolpus is named tutor of the children of Philomela, a respected and wealthy woman of Croton, who is seeking to be included in Eumolpus' will. He promptly seduces Philomela's little girl. The *Satyricon* again becomes fragmentary and concludes with the strangest **episode** of all. To his will, Eumolpus adds a clause that only those who eat part of his body after he has died will be eligible to inherit a share of his fortune. Gorgias steps forward and agrees.

Comment

Inheritance-seekers seem to have been a nuisance common to the whole Roman world. Men who rendered services of one kind or another to wealthy patrons could expect to be included in some way in their wills. Roman satirists always include inheritance-seekers in their satires, and one must ask the question whether they were a real problem or merely the subject matter of a literary **convention**. In other words, did Petronius satirize inheritance-seekers because he objected to them or because they made good material or "copy" for a story? The humorous predicaments into which Encolpius always stumbles because of his impotence had been treated some years earlier by Ovid in his *Loves* 3.7. The Romans surely never were serious worshippers of Priapus; in fact, he was almost a joke. Therefore when the god of fertility, whose statue often serves as a scarecrow, is portrayed as afflicting someone with impotence, the audience is meant to be amused and entertained. Circe, who is offended by Encolpius' impotence, is one of many domineering women in the *Satyricon*. On the other hand, many of the men are passive and abdicate the usual strong male role in favor of the female. The sexes are apparently turned around. The final scene, in which Gorgias, one of Eumolpus' heirs, agrees to eat his body, appears at first repulsive. A second look at it shows it to be funny, the sort of absurdity we have come to expect from Petronius.

THE SATYRICON

ESSAY QUESTIONS AND ANSWERS

Question: What are the two basic ingredients that go into composition of ancient fiction?

Answer: Ancient fiction is apparently a combination of a travel story, patterned originally on the *Odyssey*, and sentimental love **themes** which had become very popular in the last centuries B.C. Since study of the Odyssey was part of every student's early education, it is easy to understand its great popularity and influence. Writers of all **genres** refer to it frequently; it was the "bible" of the ancient world. Sentimental love romances appear as early as the fifth century B.C., when Euripides employs them as **theme** and structure for his later plays. Sentimental love stories are also very popular with writers of erotic poetry in Alexandria. Many basic plots for romances survive in the writings of Parthenius.

Question: What influence did historians have on ancient fiction?

Answer: From the beginnings of Greek history with Herodotus, the ancients seldom, if ever, wrote "scientific history." Facts, figures, and scientific research were unknown and even alien to their nature. Herodotus, Xenophon, and later historians preferred to write stories which illustrate and illuminate historical events, rather than report the events themselves. Much of what they wrote is based in myth or is "invented" on the slightest evidence. Their history is intended to edify and entertain, not to be a storehouse of information and research materials. Those who wrote the history of Alexander the Great described a character and events which occurred only in the minds of the writers. As these writers of "history" searched for motifs and plots which would entertain audiences, they settled on famous love stories and fabulous travel adventures. When "history" used erotic **themes** in extended digression, prose fiction was born. Thus when seeking sources, the student of the novel must always turn to the writings of ancient historians.

Question: The *Satyricon* is often referred to as a Menippean **satire**. What is a Menippean **satire**, and do any other than the *Satyricon* survive?

Answer: Menippean **satire** is a potpourri or medley of motifs, generally irreverent in nature, and written in a mixture of prose and poetry. The originator of the form, Menippus of Gadara, was a Cynic philosopher whose ideal of nil admirari (there is nothing to be admired) endeared him to Petronius. Seneca, a contemporary of Petronius, wrote a Menippean satire entitled the *Apocolocyntosis*.

Question: What is a picaresque novel, and can Encolpius be described as a "picaro"?

Answer. A picaresque novel is an adventure story, the hero or anti-hero of which is a rogue. The Spanish word "picaro" means rogue. A very popular English picaresque novel is Fielding's *Tom Jones*. The hero of these novels is not absolutely evil, nor does he act generally out of malice. Adventure, excitement, and his neighbor's wife are the usual objects of his sport. Encolpius appears to be the earliest example of what later was to be called the "picaro," a rogue or anti-hero.

Question: In what ways does the *Satyricon* reflect the social conditions of the age of Nero in which it was written?

Answer: In a general way, there can be no doubt that first-century social conditions are accurately reflected in the *Satyricon*. After several generations of peace, brought about by Augustan reform in politics and in the military, economic prosperity grew rapidly and ushered in an age of affluence previously unknown. In this age of affluence Trimalchio and many like him - poor men, former slaves, the disenfranchised - could, by hard work and a little luck, amass great fortunes. People with good business sense and the necessary daring could rise to the top. The *Satyricon* also reflects the low esteem in which organized religion was held, and the general cynicism of the intellectual class about the establishments of the Roman empire. Also, the *Satyricon* documents the great number and the influence of Greek-speaking peoples and immigrants from Asia Minor in Italy. Many small details of everyday life in ancient Italy are vividly portrayed in the speeches and actions of the individual characters.

Question: Many see the *Satyricon* as a **parody** of the *Odyssey*. What evidence is there to support this view?

Answer: There are at least three specific comparisons made in the *Satyricon* between the *Odyssey* and the action or characters in the *Satyricon*. Encolpius compares his own wanderings forced by the wrath of Priapus to the travels of Odysseus forced by Poseidon. In chapters 126ff., Encolpius, now living under the assumed name of Polyaenus, meets and falls in love with Circe.

Both Polyaenus, an epithet for Odysseus, and Circe are names taken directly from the *Odyssey*. The famous story of Odysseus' escaping the Cyclops' cave by tying himself below a sheep is parodied in chapter 97, when Giton escapes from Ascyltus by hiding under a bed in the wooly mattress. Petronius does not write a continuous or full-length **parody** of the *Odyssey*, but in certain places he imitates **episodes** from Homer, giving them a humorous twist. Every reader of the *Satyricon* could be expected to know Homer almost by heart.

Question: How does Petronius feel about the quality of education in contemporary Italy?

Answer: In first-century Italy, education and rhetoric were synonymous terms. A training in rhetoric prepared a student for work in the courts or in the Roman senate. But Rome was no longer a Republic, and an Emperor needed neither senators nor lawyers. Rhetoric, however, continued to be taught in schools and gradually supplanted all other studies. Petronius condemns this manner of education (especially in chapters 1–5) and calls for a return to the study of the old masters and for a tightening of requirements for graduation. In this discussion, as in many passages in *Satyricon*, the reader is reminded of similar controversies in the twentieth century.

Question: What is Petronius' attitude toward women in the *Satyricon*?

Answer: Women play a prominent role in the *Satyricon*, and Petronius continuously casts them as some sort of monsters. Quartilla and Oenothea, both priestesses of Priapus, are portrayed as depraved and lecherous women whose feelings run toward violence. Trimalchio's wife, Fortunata, rules her house and husband with a strong hand, and her jealousy is a starting point for marital troubles. Circe is a nymphomaniac, Philomela is willing to sell her children in exchange for inclusion in Eumolpus' will, and Pannychis, aged seven, participates in an orgy. Economic, social, and religious influences seem, in Petronius, to have produced women of only the most vulgar and debased types.

Question: What attitudes toward sex are found in the *Satyricon*?

Answer: Every one of the male characters in the *Satyricon* engages in both heterosexual and homosexual relations. Whether these relationships are one or the other, Petronius describes them in the same way, using the same language. Homosexuality in the *Satyricon* is normalcy. This attitude on the part of an individual in no way interferes with his heterosexual feelings. In chapter 127, Circe tells Encolpius that she knows about his affair with Giton and that it does not bother her. It seems that for Petronius there is no moral judgment made against homosexuality or in favor of heterosexuality. The acceptance of both practices, termed bisexuality, accurately mirrors the moral atmosphere of the day. Today such attitudes would be labeled extremely permissive; it is impossible to know for sure how they were received in ancient Italy.

Question: Who is Priapus and what is his role in the *Satyricon*?

Answer: Priapus is an Eastern fertility god who is represented as a phallus made to look like a man. In the *Satyricon* he is a comic **parody** of Homer's Poseidon. Because Encolpius offended Priapus, he is forced to wander over the Mediterranean world in search of a cure for the impotence inflicted on him by the deity.

Question: In what ways is the *Satyricon* a satire?

Answer: By **satire** we mean any type of literature directed toward the correction of vices by means of ridicule; to the Roman it meant a medley of stories. The *Satyricon* fits well into this ancient definition, and at times into the modern. Petronius does satirize Roman religion and education, poetasters, and the nouveau riche, but he is not heavy-handed or full of moralizing. The intent of his work is literary: as a literary opportunist he realizes that **satire** is easy to write because everyone can in some way identify with the satirist and against those satirized. It is a fact that men like Trimalchio make good "copy" for **satire**, and Petronius uses him and others like him merely because they provide such good material. Petronius does not come out on the side of goodness nor does he comment seriously on the great philosophical or social problems of the day. It is almost as though it were "escape literature." Actually, the best **genre** designation for the *Satyricon* is burlesque.

Question: Is the *Satyricon* obscene literature? Explain.

Answer: The *Satyricon* is hardly obscene. Its vocabulary is totally free of obscene words. A better description would be to call it erotic. There is a certain delicacy to Petronius' description of erotic scenes which keeps them from becoming obscene. At each point in the narrative when the reader might expect an obscene word or description, Petronius substitutes a harmless expression. This modus operandi becomes humorous in itself and makes otherwise obscene sections very funny.

Question: What is an interpolated tale; how does Petronius use it?

Answer: An interpolated tale is a story set inside another story. The widow of Ephesus tale (chapters 111–112) is set inside the narrative of the adventures on board ship, and is therefore interpolated. Petronius uses such tales to slow and vary the action of the main story. It is felt that the artistic quality of a work is enhanced if the pace is varied and relief from the strain of direct discourse is given: a narrator escapes the charge of preaching if he allows others to become narrators.

Question: Discuss Petronius' influence on contemporary literature.

Answer: Petronius' influence on English literature is great and seems to be increasing. Movie versions of the *Satyricon* by Fellini and Polidoro have had an important effect on present-day awareness of Petronius. The news media, especially magazines, by reporting on the *Satyricon* frequently and at length have brought it to the attention of literate society, which is now reading and studying Petronius. Christopher Fry and Stanley Silverman have each put together plays based on the *Satyricon*, and Julian Mitchell has modeled a novel on Petronius' work. Some of the truly great novelists of this century have been influenced by the *Satyricon* and recorded that influence in their writings: Lawrence Durrell, F. Scott Fitzgerald, and Aldous Huxley. The English-American poet and critic T. S. Eliot knew Petronius well and read the *Satyricon* in Latin at Harvard. With telling symbolism, Eliot uses a passage from Petronius as his superscription for *The Waste Land*. The question might well be posed: Why do moderns so much admire Petronius? A good explanation might be that modern writers and readers fell a close kinship with the Roman novelist. Like him, they live in a period of decline of old values, a period of widespread cynicism, hypocrisy, moral chaos, distrust of absolutes and generalizations. Like him, they admire the anti-hero, the man determined to survive the chaos at all costs, and they laugh at the absurdity of life in transition mainly so they will not weep. Like Petronius, the modern intellectual especially scorns the values of the middle class, and tends himself to be amoral, tolerant, and permissive in his own judgments.

BIBLIOGRAPHY

PETRONIUS: THE SATYRICON

Arrowsmith, William. *Petronius: The Satyricon.* Ann Arbor: University of Michigan Press, 1959.

Firebaugh, W. C. *The Satyricon of Petronius Arbiter.* New York: Washington Square Press (Paperback), 1966.

Heseltine, Michael, and Warmington, E. H. *Petronius: The Satyricon.* London: Heinemann, 1969 (Loeb Classical Library).

Sullivan, John. *Petronius: The Satyricon and the Fragments.* Baltimore: Penguin Books (Paperback), 1965.

PETRONIUS: CRITICISM

Auerbach, Erich. Mimesis: *The Representation of Reality in Western Literature.* Princeton: Princeton University Press (Paperback), 1948. Chapter 2: "Fortunata."

Bagnani, Gilbert. *Arbiter of Elegance: A Study of the Life and Works of C. Petronius.* Toronto: University of Toronto Press, 1954.

Corbett, Philip. *Petronius*. New York: Twayne, 1970 (Twayne's World Authors Series 97).

Perry, Ben E. *The Ancient Romances*. Berkeley: University of California Press, 1967.

Scobie, Alexander. *Aspects of the Ancient Romance and its Heritage*. Meisenheim am Glan, West Germany: Verlag Anton Hain, 1969.

Sullivan, John. *Critical Essays on Roman Literature: Satire*. Bloomington: Indiana University Press (Paperback), 1968.

Sullivan, John. *The Satyricon of Petronius: A Literary Study*. Bloomington: Indiana University Press, 1968.

Walsh, P. G. *The Roman Novel*. Cambridge: Cambridge University Press, 1970.

Wight-Duff, J. *A Literary History of Rome in the Silver Age*. London: Benn, 1964.

FIRST CENTURY ROME

Cambridge Ancient History. Vols. X-XII. Cambridge: Cambridge University Press, 1934–1939.

Cary, Max. A *History of Rome*. London: Macmillan, 1954.

Dill, Samuel. *Roman Society from Nero to Marcus Aurelius*. London: Macmillan, 1905.

Duff, A. M. *Freedmen in the Early Roman Empire*. Oxford: Oxford University Press, 1928.

Frank, Tenny. *Aspects of Social Behavior in Ancient Rome*. Cambridge, Mass.: Harvard University Press, 1932.

Lewis, N., and Reinhold, M. *Roman Civilization*. 2 Vols. New York: Harper and Row, 1951–1955.

Rostovtzeff, Michael. *Social and Economic History of the Roman Empire*. Oxford: Oxford University Press, 1963.

Syme, Ronald. *Roman Revolution*. Oxford: Oxford University Press, 1939.

PETRONIUS AND FELLINI

Fellini, Federico. *Fellini's Satyricon*. New York: Ballantine Books (Paperback), 1970. Illustrated with 80 pages of photographs from the film.

FURTHER RESEARCH

The most recent reports on Petronian scholarship will be found in the journals devoted to classical studies, especially:

Classical Bulletin, The

Classical Outlook, The

Classical World, The (For valuable surveys of Petronian scholarship, 1957–1969, see volume 62, pp. 157–164, 352–353.)

Journal of Classical Philology

Newsletter of the Petronian Society

www.ingramcontent.com/pod-product-compliance
Lightning Source LLC
LaVergne TN
LVHW011740060526
838200LV00051B/3262